GANGS

Essential Issues

GANGS

BY HAL MARCOVITZ

Content Consultant
Dennis Dressang, PhD
Professor, Public Policy and Political Science
University of Wisconsin-Madison

ABDO
Publishing Company

CREDITS

Published by ABDO Publishing Company, 8000 West 78th Street, Edina, Minnesota 55439. Copyright © 2010 by Abdo Consulting Group, Inc. International copyrights reserved in all countries. No part of this book may be reproduced in any form without written permission from the publisher. The Essential Library™ is a trademark and logo of ABDO Publishing Company.

Printed in the United States of America,
North Mankato, Minnesota
102009
012010

 PRINTED ON RECYCLED PAPER

Editor: Holly Saari
Copy Editor: Paula Lewis
Interior Design and Production: Emily Love
Cover Design: Emily Love

Library of Congress Cataloging-in-Publication Data
Marcovitz, Hal.
  Gangs / Hal Marcovitz.
      p. cm. — (Essential issues)
  Includes bibliographical references.
  ISBN 978-1-60453-954-7
  1. Gangs—United States—Juvenile literature. I. Title.
  HV6439.U5M37 2010
  364.106′60973—dc22

                                        2009029862

TABLE OF CONTENTS

Kody Scott in prison in 1993

Two Gang Members

At the age of 11, Kody Scott dropped out of school and joined the Eight Tray Gangsters. As a young gang member, Kody had to serve an apprenticeship. In the language of the streets, it meant he had to "put in work," or commit crimes and prove his toughness. At the age of 13, he robbed and assaulted a man. Kody beat him so severely he earned the nickname "Monster." "This was my 'rite of passage' to manhood," Kody later boasted.[1] "Only when I had put work in could I feel good that day."[2]

Kody Scott grew up in South Central Los Angeles, a part of the city where gangs dominate the streets. The Eight Tray Gangsters are part of the Crips, a gang network that started in South Central Los Angeles but now has sets, or smaller gangs, in many major cities.

When Kody was 16, three members of the Rollin' Sixties, a rival Crips set, cornered him on the street and shot him six times at point-blank range. Incredibly, he survived, but Kody spent weeks in a hospital recovering from the gunshot wounds.

"The name came from a beating that I had given a guy. We had robbed him, and the dude hit me in the face. Then we chased him and beat him, and stomped him and disfigured him. And the . . . police were saying, 'Whoever had did this to this cat was a monster.' And the look on people's faces when I came back to the 'hood that night— it was just power. And I felt it. And I just took the name."[3]

—Kody Scott,
on how he earned the
nickname "Monster"

Culture of Violence

By then, Kody's brother Kershaun had also joined the Eight Tray Gangsters. Kershaun, 18 months younger than Kody, had been working to prove himself every bit as tough as his older brother. On the streets, Kershaun was known as "Li'l Monster."

Kershaun felt he had to avenge his brother's shooting. He obtained a shotgun and drove into a Rollin' Sixties neighborhood with a few other members of the Eight Tray Gangsters. Soon, he saw a boy of about 14 or 15 walking by himself. The car carrying Kershaun slowed down as it approached the boy. Kershaun leaned out the window and shot the boy, killing him instantly. The victim had no connection to Kody's shooting; he was just unlucky enough to have been caught alone in Rollin' Sixties territory.

Kershaun was arrested for the shooting and sentenced to five years in juvenile detention. Kershaun served his sentence, was released, and returned to the streets. Back on Eight Tray territory, Kershaun found himself the object of much esteem by other gang members. He had committed murder, the most respected crime for a gang member.

Moreover, he had avenged the shooting of his brother, earning admiration for the Eight Trays from rival gang members. Kershaun became a dedicated gang member. He later commented,

> I would get out in the street and fight, write my name or my gang's name on the wall, I would rob you, shoot you, do whatever it took to promote my 'hood and my name. I believe my brother and I took gang-banging to another level. We lived by a creed: If you hit me, I will kill you. It wasn't get even, it was get one up. [4]

Original Gangster

After Kody recovered from the shooting, he returned to

The Writing on the Wall

In neighborhoods dominated by gangs, graffiti is more than vandalism or words painted on buildings. Graffiti is a way for gang members to mark their territory and send messages to rival gangs.

Writing graffiti is known as tagging. If a rival gang member finds himself in a South Central Los Angeles neighborhood tagged with "ETG" for Eight Tray Gangsters, he knows he is in hostile territory and should prepare for an attack or get out of the area.

According to Lou Savelli, a gang expert for the New York Police Department, graffiti is often an indication that gangs are in a neighborhood. Gangs use graffiti to send other messages, such as who has drugs to sell, which rivals are marked for murder, and which members have recently died.

Yet, graffiti is for more than criminal activities. Graffiti as an art form is gaining popularity. Graffiti artists' works are being displayed in art shows and sold at auctions in cities such as Paris, London, and New York City.

Most gang members join when they are young.

gang life and continued to live up to his nickname Monster. Soon, he graduated to status as an O.G., which means original gangster. In a gang, an O.G. heads a set, serving in a similar capacity that a senior officer would serve in the military. Kody led his

gang in continuing their criminal
activities. He said,

> Our war, like most gang wars, was
> not fought for territory or any specific
> goal other than the destruction of
> individuals, of human beings. The
> idea was to drop enough bodies, cause
> enough terror and suffering so [the other
> gangs] would come to their senses and
> we were the wrong set to [fight].[5]

Eventually, the police caught up
with Kody. In 1991, he was sentenced
to four years in prison for assault
and robbery. While in prison, Kody
converted to Islam and took the
name Sanyika Shakur. He also wrote
a memoir of his gang years titled
*Monster: The Autobiography of an L.A. Gang
Member.* Despite his vow to turn his
life around in prison, Kody has
continued to run afoul of the law.
Since serving time on the armed
robbery charge, he has been arrested
again. In 2007, he was on the Los

Gang Member Levels

Gangs have different
levels of membership.
A young gang member
or one who has not shot
anyone yet can be known
as B.G. or Baby G, which
stands for baby gangster.
A gang member can rise
through the ranks by com-
mitting crimes and violent
acts. The lead gang mem-
ber has the status of O.G.
According to Kody, there
was more to becoming
an O.G. than just being
the most violent mem-
ber of the set. The O.G.
had to build a reputation
so that he and the set
were regarded as a single
entity.

Angeles Police Department's list of "Top 10 Most Wanted Gang Members."

Breaking Away

Unlike Kody, Kershaun found a way to leave gang life. When he started a family, he realized he did not want his children to join gangs. Kershaun gave up selling cocaine, quit the Eight Trays, and entered California State University. He is now a writer who speaks out on gang-related issues and encourages young people to stay out of gangs. Kershaun said,

> For years, I had identified with what I saw in my community: the gang members, drug dealers, street hustlers and even the winos sitting in the alley.

> These were the people I saw on an everyday basis, and what they were doing became the norm. The streets and the people in it had a greater influence on my life than my mother, who was working two jobs trying to support six kids, or my father. . . . My overwhelming need to belong to something is what drew me into the Crips.[6]

A Life of Crime

Kody, however, has found it much more difficult to break away from gang life. Like Kody, many other gang members also find their futures limited because of the lifestyle they have chosen. After spending years committing smaller crimes, some graduate to bigger, more daring crimes, such as murder. Many are eventually captured by police and sentenced to lengthy prison terms. Others die in gang violence or sustain gunshot or stab wounds that cripple them for life. While some members do manage to leave gangs and make new lives for themselves, they are the exceptions.

By joining a gang, Kody and Kershaun entered a culture of violence and crime. Gang culture affects the lives of hundreds of thousands of young people in every major city in the United States and in many suburban communities and small towns. Committing robberies, assaults, and murders, and dealing drugs are common acts carried out by gang members every day.

Ice-T and Gangs

Rap star and actor Ice-T, whose real name is Tracy Marrow, said he had a loose affiliation with the Crips when he was a high school student in South Central Los Angeles. Ice-T says, "Gangbanging is something I did in high school. . . . I've never been a hard-core gang member. I'm as down as you can get, but I never put in work for a gang. . . . If you're into hard-core banging, you don't have anything else so you develop a rare and slanted grasp of life. But as people get older, they want to get out and go on with their lives and raise a family. They don't want to die in prison. If they get another chance, they quit. Gang-banging is a young man's game."[8]

Gangs have a harmful impact on U.S. society. As John S. Pistole, deputy director of the Federal Bureau of Investigation (FBI) stated, "Crime and violence are not confined to their cliques but have a chilling effect on entire communities."[7] For decades, political leaders, law enforcement officials, social workers, and others have attempted to stem the growth of youth gangs. It has been, and continues to be, a difficult task. ⌐

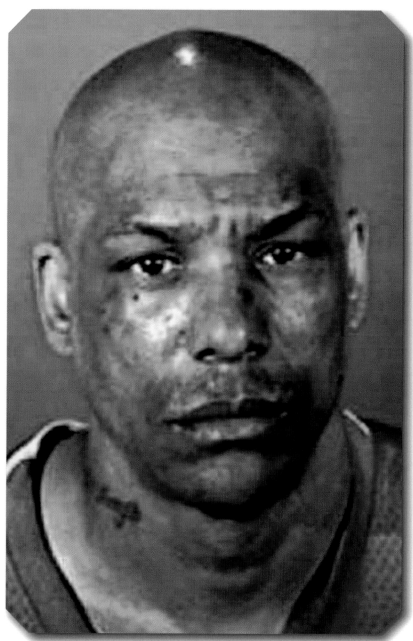

Kody Scott after being arrested for burglary in 2006

A sketch of infamous outlaw Jesse James

A History of Gangs

angs have been part of the fabric of U.S. culture since colonial times, when outlaws robbed tax collectors during the Revolutionary War. Among the most notorious were the Doans, a gang headed by brothers Levi and Abraham Doan. The

Doan brothers terrorized parts of Pennsylvania and New Jersey for approximately eight years before they were put to death by hanging.

History books are full of stories of nineteenth-century gangs that roamed the Old West. With the popularity of dime novels and silent movies in the early twentieth century, U.S. citizens soon developed romantic notions of gang life as they followed the exploits of folk heroes such as Jesse James and Billy the Kid. In the 1930s, gangs led by John Dillinger, Baby Face Nelson, and Bonnie Parker and Clyde Barrow robbed banks and made national headlines. Some stories idealized their actions. In reality, these gang leaders and other gang members were thieves and killers who often met their deaths on the run and in a shower of bullets.

The first street gang in the United States, the Forty Thieves, began around the late 1820s in New York. After the Civil War, the Five Points neighborhood in New York City swelled with tens of thousands of immigrants, many of whom were unable to find jobs. Many turned to crime, often forming gangs as a way to make money and to feel a sense of belonging. By the late 1800s, several gangs had emerged in the city.

Like modern gangs, the first street gangs were often formed along ethnic lines—there were Irish gangs, Jewish gangs, and Italian gangs. They often gave themselves memorable or sinister names, such as the Bowery Boys, Dead Rabbits, Plug Uglies, Short Tails, Slaughter Houses, and Swamp Angels. During this era, there was an average of one murder every day in the Five Points area. In the rest of New York City, there may have been one murder a month. Jacob A. Riis, a journalist and social reformer, wrote that "the gang is an institution in New York."[1]

STREET GANGS IN NEW YORK

The most notorious of the New York gangs called itself the Five Points Gang. Two Italian immigrants, Paolo Antonini Vaccarelli and Johnny Torrio, were the leaders. During the first few years of the early 1900s, the Five Points Gang and its rivals

Five Points

The Lower Manhattan neighborhood known as Five Points spanned a five-square-block area centered at the intersection of what are now Park, Worth, and Orange streets. Most families were crowded into one- or two-room apartments in ramshackle tenements. Plumbing was inadequate and raw sewage often pooled in the streets. Pigs, rats, and other vermin ran wild.

A run-down neighborhood in New York City in 1968

committed a wide range of street crimes—burglaries, assaults, armed holdups, and swindles. Their activities changed on January 16, 1920—the date the Eighteenth Amendment to the U.S. Constitution established Prohibition. The amendment outlawed alcoholic beverages in the United States. Overnight, gangs gave up their petty criminal activities for the far more lucrative enterprise of bootlegging, the making and selling of illegal alcohol.

Prohibition lasted 13 years. During that time, gangs turned into major mobs earning millions of dollars a year. One-time street hoodlums such as Al Capone and Charlie "Lucky" Luciano became millionaire bootleggers. Eventually, they would establish *La Cosa Nostra*, the Sicilian criminal network also known as the Mafia. These men would elevate gang culture into big business. When Prohibition was repealed in 1933,

On to Larger Crimes

Some of the most powerful mobsters of the 1930s, 1940s, and 1950s started out as members of a street gang headed by Charlie "Lucky" Luciano. Three of these gang members were Meyer Lansky, Benny "Bugsy" Siegel, and Frank Costello. At first, Luciano's gang committed stickups, burglaries, and other small-time crimes, but bigger crimes were ahead. Eventually, Luciano became in charge of all rackets in New York. Then, in 1936, he was sent to prison on the charge of organizing a prostitution ring.

After World War II, Siegel and Lansky built the first casino-hotel in Las Vegas, Nevada. They used mob money to finance the venture. When Siegel was caught stealing from the mob, he was murdered. Lansky opened casinos in Havana, Cuba. In 1959, Fidel Castro took control of the country and put his men in charge of the casinos. Lansky was kicked out and returned to the United States. Federal agents hounded him until his death in 1983.

Costello eventually headed one of the biggest illegal gambling operations in the United States. He gave up the business in 1957 after a rival gangster made an unsuccessful attempt on his life.

they moved on to other criminal enterprises, such as illegal drug trafficking, gambling, and prostitution. Today, elements of *La Cosa Nostra* continue to exist in some U.S. cities.

While higher levels of organized crime became big business, the streets across the country were left to young hoodlums. Many formed gangs along ethnic lines. African Americans formed gangs in Los Angeles as early as the 1920s, particularly in the neighborhoods of Watts and East Los Angeles. They took names such as the Magnificents and the Driver Brothers.

Latino gangs formed in many big cities, particularly Los Angeles, Chicago, and New York. During the early part of the century, Latinos and their families fled the Mexican Revolution and moved into large U.S. cities. Some Latino teenagers formed gangs. Many of the Latino gang members dressed in flashy clothes known as zoot suits. They hung around Los Angeles streets. At night they would often assault passersby or pull knives on sailors who were on shore leave.

For months, racial hostility between the Latino gang members and the white sailors simmered. On June 3, 1943, the volatile situation erupted into five days of lawlessness and riots. Latinos, whether they were gang members or not, were assaulted by white sailors and others. During the so-called zoot suit riots, hundreds of young Latinos were beaten up while hundreds more were dragged off by police. The riots finally died down after the U.S. Navy declared Los Angeles off-limits to all sailors.

Gangs Continue

The rioting did not eliminate the gangs in Los Angeles or elsewhere. African-American gangs were growing. By the 1970s, the most powerful gang on Los Angeles streets was the Crips, a primarily African-American gang.

Latino gangs were also growing. In the 1980s, young Salvadorans fled their country to escape civil war. These young immigrants established one of the most powerful Latino gangs, *Mara Salvatrucha.* This gang

"Marching through the streets of downtown Los Angeles, a mob of several thousand soldiers, sailors, and civilians proceeded to beat up every zoot suiter they could find. Pushing its way into the important motion picture theaters, the mob ordered the management to turn on the house lights and then [moved] up and down the aisles, dragging Mexicans out of their seats. Streetcars were halted while Mexicans, and some Filipinos and Negroes, were jerked out of their seats, pushed into the street, and beaten with sadistic frenzy."[2]

—Carey McWilliams, journalist and witness to the zoot suit riots was originally composed of youths only from El Salvador. Now, the gang includes young people from several Central and South American countries, including Honduras and Guatemala.

Asians from Vietnam, Cambodia, Laos, the Philippines, South Korea, and other countries have formed gangs as well. Two of the largest Asian gangs are the Asian Boyz and the Tiny Rascals.

White youths have also formed gangs, but they are often prompted more by racial hatred than a desire to organize criminal activities in their neighborhoods. They often form white-supremacy or neo-Nazi groups.

While gangs have been around since the early twentieth century, membership has gone through substantial change. During the rise of organized crime in the twentieth century, gangs comprised primarily

Posing as Heroes

Even a century ago, gang members regarded themselves as local heroes, especially if they had been arrested. Journalist and social reformer Jacob A. Riis wrote that getting arrested raised a gang member's social standing. Riis said that all gangs have a "common [program]: to get . . . arrested, so as to pose as heroes before their fellows."[3]

Nazi Low Riders

One of the largest neo-Nazi youth gangs is the Nazi Low Riders, which was formed in the 1970s in California. Since then, the group has expanded into Arizona, Colorado, Florida, and Illinois. According to the Anti-Defamation League, which monitors hate groups, the Nazi Low Riders commit racially motivated violent acts.

adult members. Today, gangs are primarily youth-driven with members as young as ten years old. Some gangs have grown into powerful organizations, but all gangs continue to be a challenge for communities and law enforcement groups in the United States. Yet the makeup of gangs has changed substantially. ⌐

A police officer speaking to members of a white-supremacist gang

Three members of the Bloods being arrested in 2007

GANG NETWORKS

oday, gangs are organized similar to military units. They have leaders, soldiers, and new recruits. Their members wear uniforms of a sort, communicate in code, and carry arms. If authorities find a way to imprison the leader, or if the leader is killed in a dispute with a rival gang, the gang does not dissolve. Someone within the ranks of the gang takes command. A member of the Gangster Disciples compared the group's staying power to the operation of a circus: "We're going to miss him, but we still must go on. The show must go on. It's like the circus. The show must go on."[1]

Some gangs have grown into national organizations and networks. They are not administered by a single national leader or ruling body, but they may have sets in a number of towns and cities. They may be loosely affiliated or may even be rivals.

CRIPS AND BLOODS

Crips and Bloods are among the most notorious and largest of gangs, with sets in cities across the United States. The Crips originated in 1969 by Raymond Washington, a member of a gang in South Central

Gang Growth

According to a 2009 FBI report, gang membership is continuing to grow. In 2005, there were an estimated 800,000 gang members in the United States. As of September 2008, gang membership was estimated at 1 million, with approximately 20,000 gangs.

Los Angeles known as the Avenues. The Avenues were affiliated with the Black Panther Party, which maintained a violent political agenda. In 1969, Los Angeles Panther leaders were killed in a gun battle with FBI agents, and many of the group's gang affiliations dissolved. Washington invited former Panther affiliates to join his new gang. First called the Baby Avenues and then Baby Cribs, the gang evolved into the Crips. In 1971, another gang leader, Stanley "Tookie" Williams, merged his gang with Washington's. In 2009, there may have been as many as 35,000 Crips in the United States, with sets in most major cities.

By the late 1970s, a second gang had emerged in Southern California to challenge the Crips. The Bloods were born on the streets of Compton, a suburb of Los Angeles. In 2009, the Bloods had as many as 20,000 members.

Gang Identification

Gangs can use clothing to identify fellow members and rivals. Several gangs in one territory may wear certain colors to differentiate themselves from other gangs. For example, one gang may wear red and its rival may wear blue. Wearing a gang color could be as subtle as tying a shoe with one red shoelace.

Gang graffiti in a New York City suburb

The hatred between Crips and Bloods is deep. For years, fights have broken out between them. Probably thousands of Crips and Bloods have died in brawls over the decades.

LATINO GANGS

Many gangs have developed in the United States among ethnic and immigrant groups. Members may join these gangs for protection and a sense of belonging in an unfamiliar place.

One such gang is Mara Salvatrucha, which includes 8,000 to 10,000 members in 38 states. The gang operates worldwide with an estimated 30,000 to 50,000 total members. Mara Salvatrucha has something of a national hierarchy— members from Los Angeles are more highly regarded than members from other cities. The head of a local Mara Salvatrucha gang is known as the *ranflero*, or "shot-caller."

Another Latino gang is the 18th Street gang. The gang originated at the intersection of 18th Street and Union Avenue in Los Angeles. It is one of the largest Latino-based gangs in the United States, with as many as

Mara Salvatrucha

The Latino gang Mara Salvatrucha draws its name from two sources. *La Mara* is a violent street gang in El Salvador. *Salvatruchas* were members of a political party that was formerly a communist guerilla movement in El Salvador. Gang members admire the Salvatruchas not because of their political ideology, but because of their courage and relentless use of violence to smash their enemies. The gang frequently abbreviates its name as MS-13, which refers to the 13 original members of a gang known as the Mexican Mafia.

A police officer searching members of the 18th Street gang in 1987

50,000 members, including 7,000 in Los Angeles. 18th Street gang sets have been identified as far east as Washington DC.

Sur 13 is a Latino gang that maintains close ties to organized crime leaders in Mexico. Short for *Los Sureños*, the Spanish term for "the Southerners," Sur 13 sells drugs smuggled into the United States by

Mexican drug traffickers. Rivals of Los Sureños are *Los Norteños*, or "the Northerners."

In the Midwest, Chicago has spawned two prominent gangs: the Latin Kings and the Vice Lords. Established by Puerto Rican youths, the Latin Kings include as many as 50,000 followers in 34 states, but about half are believed to be living in the Chicago area.

The Vice Lords is an African-American gang. Vice Lords sets have been established outside Chicago in at least 28 states. Membership is approximately 35,000.

Asian Gangs

In 1975, the long and devastating Vietnam War in Southeast

Cyber Gangs

Recently, gangs have started communicating through the Internet. The Internet is often used as a substitute for more traditional means of harassment, such as graffiti and face-to-face interactions. Gang members also use the Internet to communicate with fellow members. Using social networking sites and personal Web pages, gangs recruit new members, post threats to rivals, and brag about their criminal exploits.

Threats over the Internet can escalate into real-life violence. San Mateo, California, Police Chief Susan Manheimer said, "We'll see something start on the Internet and actually turn into an assault or a gang fight that actually results out of Internet profiling."[2]

Authorities are following gang Internet use to investigate criminal activity. Chicago police arrested an adolescent male after they linked his MySpace page to a graffiti crime at a church. Law enforcement officials are also studying gang sites to learn more about the gangs.

Asia ended when communist troops flooded into South Vietnam. Thousands of Vietnamese families fled the communist regime. Families from neighboring Laos and Cambodia also fled brutal and bloodthirsty regimes. Many of them made their way to Long Beach, California. By the 1980s, Long Beach had become the headquarters for the Asian Boyz, a gang composed of young refugees from Southeast Asian countries.

Another Asian gang is the Tiny Rascals, which is a rival of the Asian Boyz. The Tiny Rascals are composed of Cambodian immigrants and have members on the East Coast, particularly cities in New England.

Clearly, many gangs have endured for decades. While some gangs were established to protect their members, most have expanded to include criminal activities. The larger, more notorious gangs have survived

Tookie Williams

In 1981, Crips leader Stanley "Tookie" Williams was convicted of the murders of a store clerk and three members of a family who owned a Los Angeles motel. Though he was sentenced to death, Williams maintained his innocence. While in prison, Williams turned his life around—he wrote a children's book titled *Tookie Speaks Out Against Gang Violence*. All profits were donated to antigang programs. He also wrote two books for older readers denouncing gang violence and, in 2004, when a war broke out between Crips and Bloods, he helped broker a peace from his jail cell.

As the date of his execution approached, many people called for California Governor Arnold Schwarzenegger to grant clemency, or provide leniency, to Williams. The governor refused, insisting that Williams had never shown remorse for the murders. In 2005, Williams was executed after spending 24 years on death row.

great turnovers in their memberships as members have been killed, gone to prison, or left. And yet the gangs have survived, becoming influential and destructive forces in their communities.

Former Crips leader Stanley "Tookie" Williams was executed in 2005.

*A group of reported gang members walking down an alley
in Los Angeles, California, in 1987*

WHY YOUNG PEOPLE
JOIN GANGS

Many members say the allure of being in a gang is about more than just the desire to earn easy money and establish a tough reputation. Many gang members have absent fathers, and other family members may be dead, in jail, or addicted to drugs. Lacking any semblance of normal family lives, many young people say the primary draw of gangs is the closeness between members. "The gang was really my family because my family was not there," said Vincent Castro, a former gang member from Santa Barbara, California.[1]

In functioning family homes, parents or guardians guide young people through early life. These adults know the differences between right and wrong and help their sons and daughters make the right decisions. When such an adult is missing, a gang leader may fill in as a parental figure. However, his or her guidance does not help the young members make decisions about what is right and what is wrong.

Gangs can estrange members from their own families, as California Attorney General Edmund G. Brown Jr. reported,

Once a child is lost to a gang, it is hard to get him or her back because the gang can literally become a surrogate

Society's Rules Do Not Apply

The Justice Policy Institute is a Washington-based organization that studies criminal justice issues. In 2007, the group issued a report that stated, "What distinguishes the most deeply involved gang members from peers is a worldview in which fighting is a normal part of life and the rules of mainstream society do not fully apply."[2]

family for that young person. The loyalties, love and dedication normally found in traditional nuclear families are transferred to the gang family. Members can develop these intense bonds with other members and feel a need to protect them. Many times, problems at home act as a cohesive factor for gang members. [3]

Gang Membership

The lack of strong family support is only one of many reasons young people join gangs. If a young person lives in a gang-infested neighborhood, the question may not be whether to join a gang, but which gang to join. "Contrary to popular belief, I didn't join because I lacked a family," said Vice Lords member Albert McGee.

For me, it was simply a matter of my surroundings. Had I lived about four blocks over, I would've been a Black Gangster Disciple instead of [a] . . . Vice Lord. [4]

Young people also join gangs because they are doing poorly in school, their friends may already be gang members, their families may live in poverty, or they may be using drugs.

Most gang members join at very young ages—ten or eleven is not an unusual age to join. Some

Children may join gangs because their friends are already members or because they are doing poorly in school.

may join at even younger ages. Sociologists have determined that the age of initiation into gangs has not changed that much over the decades. Entry into gang life has always started early. Former University of Southern California sociologist Malcolm W. Klein stated,

> For many decades, the initial entry into gangs has been at around eleven years of age. . . . Although some writers and officials decry the eight- and ten-year-old gang member, they haven't been in the business long enough to realize that we heard the same reports twenty and forty years ago.[5]

Money and a Reputation

There is no question that lack of family, heavy gang presence in the neighborhood, and other social ills greatly influence a young person's decision to join a gang. But many gang members admit they were drawn by the lure of money and a tough reputation. They may think that with a reputation they can attract the opposite sex and with money they can buy expensive jewelry, cars, and other luxuries. Kody Scott said,

There's a lot of talk about loyalty and mission and all that with the gang, and that's part of it. But my initial attraction to these guys I saw who were in gang life was that these dudes

---

Gang Initiation

To join a gang, a potential member may have to go through a process called "jumping in." This means he lets himself be beaten up by other gang members to prove his toughness. Former Crip Colton Simpson described the day he was jumped in by his gang:

Kicked in the stomach, the wind is knocked out of me. I gasp and force my eyes to center. . . . The world swims as I receive another kick and a strike. Hard spitting-punches come from all angles. I'm tossed by blows like a speed-punching bag. They have the control. Stars swim before my eyes again.[6]

Standing up to a beating is considered a test of loyalty, but there are other ways to join a gang. An established gang member can sponsor a friend. By vouching for the new member, the existing member eliminates the need for a jumping in. Another way of joining is to commit a crime on the orders of the gang. The crime can range from marking the gang's territory with graffiti to committing murder.

---

were ghetto stars. And I wanted to be a ghetto star.[7]

SEEKING PROTECTION

Another reason young people join gangs is for protection—a young boy may feel threatened by a gang and will join a rival gang to protect himself. This is particularly important for drug dealers. If their business is lucrative, drug dealers can find themselves victims of violent attacks by gang members who try to steal their money and drugs. Cory, a 16-year-old gang member from Los Angeles, said,

> *Man I joined the Fultons because there are a lot of people out there who are trying to get you and if you don't got protection you in trouble sometimes. My homeboys gave me protection, so hey, they were the thing to do. . . . Now that I got some business things going I can concentrate on them and not worry so much. I don't*

Blood In, Blood Out

Police in Ashland, Massachusetts, arrested two men in 2007 for participating in a Bloods gang initiation ritual. During the ritual, the men assaulted a victim with knives. Only by drawing another person's blood could the men join the gang, police said. The gang maintained a "blood in, blood out" policy, meaning they had to shed someone's blood in order to join or quit the gang.

Ashland police detective Greg Fawkes said the gang members approached the victim and ordered him to turn over his wallet, then slashed him with their knives. One police officer said, "I don't think they were interested in his money—they all had to get their swipes in to shed his blood to gain membership to the gang. Had he not put his hands up, it would have been his face that got slashed."[8] The victim survived the attack.

always have to be looking over my shoulder.[9]

**Demographics
of Gang Members**

According to a 2007 study by the National Youth Gang Center of Washington DC, nearly 50 percent of gang members are Latinos and 35 percent are African Americans. Whites, Asians, and members of other ethnic groups compose the remainder of gang membership.

FEMALE MEMBERS

While most gang members are male, there are female gang members too. There are also all-female gangs, which may or may not be linked to a male gang. A 2007 study found that females comprise approximately 10 percent of the membership of street gangs in the United States.

Females join gangs for many reasons. They may seek financial security or friendship. They may join along ethnic lines. They may be looking for escape from troubles at home, as many females who join gangs have been sexually abused. However, female gang members usually quit gangs earlier than male members, sometimes as a result of pregnancy.

Female gangs are usually less delinquent than their male counterparts. Their criminal activities range from property crimes to drug dealing.

Police arrested this female, a suspected member of the Crips, in 2007.

A police gang unit at the scene of a gang-related shooting in 2007

GANGS AND CRIME

angs are notorious for their criminal
activities. The number-one criminal
enterprise of street gangs is the distribution of
illegal drugs. In some areas, local law enforcements
report that gangs are responsible for approximately

80 percent of drug crimes. Gang members usually serve as low-level dealers, selling marijuana, crack cocaine, and other drugs directly to users.

DRUG DISTRIBUTORS

The National Alliance of Gang Investigators Associations (NAGIA) conducted a survey of law enforcement officials. The results showed that street gang members are the primary distributors of illegal drugs in the United States. Street gangs sell 65 percent of the nation's marijuana as well as 47 percent of crack cocaine and 39 percent of crystal methamphetamine. They also sell powdered cocaine, heroin, and ecstasy.

Selling drugs can be dangerous, and gang members who do so lead violent lives. According to the NAGIA survey, robbery and aggravated assault are two crimes

Gang Members Brag

Usually when people commit crimes, they try to keep quiet about them. After all, criminals have a better chance of getting away with their crimes if no one knows they are responsible. But gang members brag about their crimes in order to gain respect in the eyes of other gang members. "If a member never speaks about any of his . . . crimes, the member will never be noticed by the gang," say gang experts Derrick Watkins and Richard Ashby. "Bragging about the crimes committed, particularly violent crimes, creates an image for the member within the gang as well as within the local neighborhood."[1]

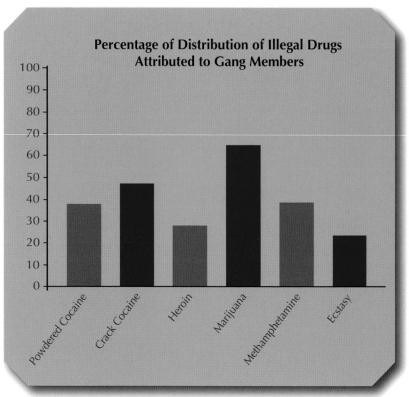

Percentage of Distribution of Illegal Drugs Attributed to Gang Members

Gang involvement in U.S. drug sales in 2005

closely associated with drug dealing by gang members.

Gang leaders also get involved in drug trafficking, serving as midlevel distributors who supply the street dealers in their gangs with drugs. But gang members rarely rise to the higher levels of the illegal drug business. Drug trafficking is largely controlled by foreign kingpins who smuggle drugs across the Mexican or Canadian borders. Drug kingpins in Mexico supply most of the drugs peddled by the Latino street gangs of Southern California.

Some Asian street gangs have struck alliances with organized crime groups in Asian nations. Many Asian drug lords operate in the Golden Triangle, a region that encompasses portions of Myanmar, Thailand, Laos, and Vietnam. Crime groups in Asia have made contacts with the Asian Boyz, the Tiny Rascals, and other Asian gangs in the United States, enlisting the gang members as street dealers.

Drug Users

Many gang members not only sell drugs, but they use drugs themselves. They may use marijuana or harder drugs as a form of recreation or as a way of finding the courage to commit

National Gang Intelligence Center

In 2005, the FBI established the National Gang Intelligence Center (NGIC) as a central agency to fight gangs in all regions of the United States. The NGIC works with federal, state, and local law enforcement groups to provide intelligence and tactics that decrease and prevent gang activity.

crimes. Twace, a Latino gang member from New York, stated,

> *I started popping pills like crazy. . . . I mean, I didn't even know what I was on, I was so wiped out of my head. I just did it because I liked the way I looked when I was high—I looked like I was a maniac, I looked like I was crazy.*[2]

Twace said he used drugs to earn respect. He knew nobody would want to fight him if they knew he could lash out in a drug-induced frenzy. Twace said he started taking methaqualone, a type of illegal drug, when he was 13 years old. By the

Gangsta Rap

Rap music emerged in the United States in the 1970s. In 1989, the genre changed drastically when the rap group NWA released the album *Straight Outta Compton*. The album's hard-hitting pieces advocated violence and gangs. It helped launch the genre known as gangsta rap.

Some of gangsta rap's biggest stars are former gang members. Calvin Broadus Jr.—known to his fans as Snoop Dogg—was a Crip. Marion "Suge" Knight is the cofounder of Death Row Records, which produced many gangsta rap hits in the 1990s. Before becoming a music executive, Knight was a member of the Bloods.

Gang members have embraced gangsta rap as their culture's poetry, a way of telling their stories in their own language. John M. Hagedorn, author of *A World of Gangs: Armed Young Men and Gangsta Culture*, wrote,

> *The popularity of gangsta rap comes from its ironic and defiant nature, its hardcore beats, and its very negativity in a world that appears unchangeable. . . . [Gangsta rapper] Ice-T adds: "The music isn't supposed to be positive. It's supposed to be negative, because the streets are negative."*[3]

time he was 15, he had graduated to heroin. By the age of 21, Twace had quit his gang and was in drug rehabilitation.

OTHER CRIMES

Gangs also commit crimes unrelated to drugs. Sometimes the crimes are between gangs. Gang members may rob rival gang members or assault them. Disputes between gangs are often settled in gunfights.

Gang members also commit crimes against the larger community. Thefts of cars, firearms, jewelry, and credit cards have become big businesses for gang members. Colton Simpson, a former member of the Rollin' Thirties, a Crips set, once robbed a Los Angeles jewelry store with two fellow gang members. It took the three members no more than a few minutes to rob the jewelry store of $150,000.

Killing for Money

In an interview with National Public Radio, a former Latino gang member known as El Cholo explained the violent world of his gang: "When I joined the Bikingo gang, they taught me how to use weapons and be in a gang. Later, I joined Mara 13, the Salvatrucha. I was with them. I learned how to survive there.

"There are lots of gangs and how they survive is *asesino al sueldo*, kill for a paycheck. A person who needs money has to kill another person. They come, kill a person, take his money and that's how they survive. Or they survive violating people, kill them, kidnap them, assault banks, rob people in the street, and sell drugs. That's what gangs do, and I did it, too."[4]

Los Angeles police searched and questioned three suspected gang members near a playground in 2007.

When armed gang members commit a crime, there is a good chance it will turn violent. According to the U.S. Justice Department, between 1993 and 2003, street gang members committed 373,000 violent crimes, or 6 percent of all violent crimes in the United States. Such acts included rape and sexual assault, robbery, and assault.

Murder

The Justice Department also reported that gang members committed 6.5 percent of all murders in the United States in 2003. This included 9.3 percent—nearly one in ten—of all murders committed with guns.

Perhaps one reason murder rates are high is because gang members easily obtain guns and regularly carry them. Also, killing is thought to be an acceptable method of resolving disputes. Kody Scott obtained his first gun at the age of 14. It was not long before he used it in a confrontation with a rival gang member.

Scott recalled,

> [A rival] leapt from the car, circled from the front, walked up, and hit me in the mouth. . . . I knew I needed an equalizer, because he lifted his shirt to reveal the butt of a pistol in his waistband. I turned and bolted. Running at top speed with tears streaming down my face, I made my way back home, went right in, got my gun, and trotted back to the bus stop.

A Narrow Escape

Kody Scott once joined a fight to help his brother. Knocked to the ground and disoriented, Scott drew his gun and fired, but nothing happened— it wasn't loaded. Only then did Scott realize he had pointed the gun at his mother. She had hurried over to try to break up the fight.

I was hoping the bus hadn't come, so that the three girls who saw me get hit could watch me kill him.[5]

Scott approached his rival's home and fired six shots from his gun, hoping to kill the gang member. He did not, but Scott was caught the next day and spent 60 days in juvenile hall for the crime.

FBI agents entering an apartment building to arrest gang members on drug charges

Law enforcement officials and emergency responders at the scene of a gang-related shooting in the rural town of Dodge City, Kansas

GANGS OUTSIDE BIG CITIES

The Yakima Valley in central Washington State may not seem a likely place to find gangs. However, in 2000, police estimated that about 1,400 gang members lived in Yakima, a small city with a population of approximately 70,000 at the time. Another 1,400 gang members were believed to live in nearby communities.

In the Washington towns of Yakima, Sunnyside, Grandview, Centralia, and Union Gap, buildings have been tagged with insignias, mottos, and other forms of gang graffiti. It is not unusual for people who live in the Yakima Valley to endure drive-by shootings, murders, assaults, and drug crimes. These types of crimes were previously known mostly in the gang-infested neighborhoods of the big cities. "I'm just tired of it already," said Israel Yanez, a Sunnyside father of five whose neighborhood has been the scene of two drive-by shootings. "I'm pretty sure everybody else is tired of it, too."[1]

Experts say the spread of gangs outside of cities was inevitable. As families seek employment opportunities, many migrate to

Less Drug Competition

The growth of gangs in small towns may have to do with less competition between drug dealers. Because there are fewer drug dealers in rural areas, gang members do not worry about losing their customers to the competition. They know they can earn bigger profits than on city street corners. "It's all price driven," says Jim Wright of the Minnesota Gang Strike Force in Duluth. "If you can drive five or six hours and make five times more money, you're going to do it."[2]

The rural area of Yakima Valley in Washington State has seen a rise in gang activity.

suburbs and small towns. Some families bring their gang ties with them. "What we are seeing is a migration of gangs from larger cities . . . to more rural areas," says Jerry Hunter, head of an antigang unit for the California Attorney General's Office. "The gang activity . . . is a huge crisis for those communities."[3]

SMALL-TOWN GANGS

Law enforcement officials and civic leaders find it particularly troubling that the gangs establishing themselves in smaller communities are the same ones that have dominated the inner-city streets. The Crips, the Bloods, the Mara Salvatrucha, and others have brought their culture and rituals, which are largely based on criminal activities, violence, and domination over the enemies. Rival gangs in large cities have become rival gangs in small towns.

However, small-town gangs differ from larger ones in that they are often confined to a specific group of young people. As these young people grow older or leave the area, the gang may diminish.

Because gangs are new in small towns, the general community is still trying to find an appropriate response to the problem. In Red Bluff, a tiny town in California's Central Valley, a 17-year-old gang member from Los Sureños was sentenced to 25 years in prison

Antigang Ordinance

To deal with its gang problem, the town council of Sunnyside, Washington, passed an antigang ordinance in 2007. This made it illegal to join a gang and gave police the power to arrest gang members simply for wearing gang colors. Civil rights supporters declared the law unconstitutional. They insisted that police do not have the power to arrest someone simply for wearing red or blue clothes.

Advised that the cases would not hold up in court, Sunnyside police have never arrested gang members based on their clothes. Still, the ordinance has been effective. Authorities in the town say gang activity has decreased.

after shooting a member of the Los Norteños gang during a party. "This is a small town and . . . we're not used to those type of things happening," said Greg Ulloa, chief of juvenile probation in Tehama County.[4]

Small towns may also be ill-equipped to handle gang activity. Their police departments may not have enough officers, and the officers may not be properly trained to confront the unique problems of controlling gang violence. In Greeley, Colorado, a small city with a population of 80,000, six homicides were committed in 2004. All were gang related. Another 26 people sustained gunshot wounds—all in gang-related cases. Initially, Greeley police had a difficult time controlling the gang violence in the area. Eventually, the police department doubled the size of its gang unit and assigned three detectives exclusively to gang-related cases. With the

A Year in Jail for Graffiti

Outdoor walls in large city neighborhoods are often covered with gang-related graffiti. But in small towns, authorities are far less tolerant of such vandalism. In Yakima, Washington, two members of what police described as a "tagging crew" were each sentenced to a year in jail for painting graffiti on a number of local businesses. (Tagging crews are similar to gangs—they often fight violent territory wars over the rights to tag a neighborhood with graffiti.) Judge Michael McCarthy came down hard on defendants Dennis Rose and Brandon Syverson. Rose's attorney, Ulvar Klein, believed it was the first time anyone in Yakima has gone to prison for graffiti.

expanded workforce, the violence in Greeley receded.

While Greeley may have found a measure of control over its gang problem, nearby towns continue to struggle with it. Next to Greeley, the small town of Evans has seen a growth in gang-related crime. Each year, police in this town of 19,000 people respond to approximately 50 gang-related calls. Police suspect that most of the gang members are from Greeley.

Like Evans, many small towns receive spillover gang activity from nearby larger communities that have taken steps to eradicate gangs. In Covington, Tennessee, police blame their gang problem on a crackdown on gang activity in the nearby city of Memphis. Labeled "Blue Crush," the Memphis crackdown rounded up dozens of gang members with outstanding warrants. Once other gang members learned of the

Territory Wars outside Cities

Authorities see gang wars occurring outside big cities. John P. Moore, director of the National Youth Gang Center, states, "In areas where suburbs are close and similar to cities, these gangs really prowl around a lot. The old image of territoriality is not what it used to be. They're mobile; they're going to move around and do things. And they're going to run into other gangs, which is when the violence usually begins."[5]

roundup, many fled to nearby towns, including Covington, where they have worked to reestablish their territories. Covington's population is just 9,000, but local police have arrested Crips, Bloods, Vice Lords, and Gangster Disciples.

Gangs in the Suburbs

Even in suburban residential areas, gang activity has surfaced. In White Plains, New York, police arrested nine members of the *Treces Locos* gang for beating a victim to death. Gang members have also been identified in other affluent New York communities, such as Port Chester, Westchester, and Sleepy Hollow. In Port Chester, for example, police arrested 30 members of the *La Clica* gang, mostly for petty crimes. According to Port Chester police, gang members seem most interested in smoking marijuana, consuming alcohol, and harassing citizens of the small community.

Suburban gang members do more than just harass people, however. Members of the Fluffy Bunny Crew in Arizona have dealt drugs and committed armed robberies. "These guys are moving more and more into traditional gang crimes," says Jim Hill, a gang investigator with the

---

Arizona Department of Public Safety. "We have drug transactions on a regular basis."[6]

In 2006, the class president of Harry S. Truman High School in suburban Philadelphia was unable to accept his diploma with other students because police believed the Bloods would try to kill him. Tyrone Lewis had done nothing to the Bloods. However, his sister had agreed to be a witness against gang members in a New Jersey murder trial. In retaliation, the Bloods threatened the life of her brother.

Lewis was still allowed to give his commencement speech. He made his speech from an undisclosed

Affluent Gangs

Gangs composed of affluent youths in middle- and upper-class neighborhoods have confounded police for many years. Some gangs are unaffiliated with inner-city street gangs. Usually they form among friends who are not seeking ways to make money or establish tough reputations. Rather, most of these gang members are bored and seek thrills.

Their crimes range from petty vandalism to violent acts. In affluent Yorktown, New York, members of the Benzi Boyz gang took their name from the expensive Mercedes-Benz automobiles they vandalized. To gain entry into the gang, a potential member was required to break off a Mercedes-Benz hood ornament and wear it on a chain around his neck.

Law enforcement officials say that many affluent parents refuse to believe their children become involved in gang-related activities. "Some of these parents question what we've done instead of questioning what their kid has done," says Karyn Addison, a detective in upscale Mount Vernon, New York. "Instead of, 'My God, my son has a gun,' it's 'How can you prove he had a gun?'"[7]

location, where it was televised by satellite to the Truman commencement. James Drum, a parent who attended the commencement, said, "You hear about gangs occasionally and you worry about it all the time. The thing you worry about most is the cross fire. Your kid's in the wrong place at the wrong time, and it's all over."[8]

Graffiti can be a sign of gang activity in a neighborhood.

*A memorial for Jamiel Shaw, who was shot
and killed by gang members in 2008*

THE CONSEQUENCES
OF GANGS

*J*amiel Shaw completed his junior season
on his high school football team in 2007.
Coaches from major colleges had been in contact
with the young running back, and they promised
to stay in touch with him during his senior year.

Jamiel was sure that he was on track for a college scholarship. His future looked bright.

But as he walked home one night in March 2008, a car pulled alongside him. Inside the car were members of the 18th Street gang. One of the gang members asked Jamiel which gang he belonged to. Before Jamiel had a chance to answer, a gang member drew a gun and shot Jamiel twice in the head, killing him instantly. Jamiel's friends and family were devastated, and his death was an incredible loss for the community. "A kid like that doesn't come around too often," said Jamiel's football coach, Hardy Williams.[1]

There is no question that Jamiel's Los Angeles neighborhood was infested with gangs. The Bloods had dominated the neighborhood. But in recent years, members of the 18th Street gang had been challenging the Bloods in their territory. Had the killer waited for Jamiel to answer his question, he would have learned that Jamiel was not his enemy. He was not a Blood. In fact, he was not a member of any gang.

The death of Jamiel Shaw illustrates the true consequence of gangs—the loss of bright young people. Indeed, the futures of two young men were lost the night Jamiel died. Soon after the shooting, police tracked down the alleged killer, 19-year-old Pedro Espinoza. If found guilty of Jamiel's murder, Espinoza could face the death penalty.

In addition to the actual crimes, gangs spread terror that resonates throughout an entire community. People who live around gangs live in fear. Gangs also prevent neighborhoods from prospering. Because of the likelihood that they would be robbed or vandalized, businesses do not want to invest in gang territories. For this reason,

The Gangs of Hollenbeck

Hollenbeck, a neighborhood in East Los Angeles, is regarded as one of the most gang-infested neighborhoods in the United States. According to the Los Angeles police department, 34 gangs fight for territory in the neighborhood. In 2003, membership in those gangs was estimated at 6,800 young people—3.5 percent of Hollenbeck's population.

Fearing the gangs, new businesses are leery to open in Hollenbeck, and established businesses leave. As a result, nearly one-third of Hollenbeck families live below the poverty line. In 2007, the unemployment rate in the neighborhood was more than 10 percent—twice the national average at the time. According to police, more than 700 gang-related crimes are reported in Hollenbeck each year.

Nearly every family in Hollenbeck has been touched by gang violence. Hollenbeck resident Soledad Brock lost both her sons to gang murders. One son, Angel, joined the State Street gang. The other, Ronny, resisted gang life and joined the U.S. Marines. Just before leaving for duty, he was gunned down on the street. Months after his brother's death, Angel was approached by rival gang members and shot to death on the front porch of his home.

unemployment often is high in areas of gang activity, which leads to poverty.

Effect on Education

Gangs can have a particularly devastating impact on schools. It is not unusual for young gang members to carry out their territory battles in hallways or schoolyards. When gang activity shows up in schools, drugs and guns often accompany it.

In Salem, Oregon, teachers often can identify current or potential gang members by their poor performances in school. Gang members often read two or three grades below their level. Eduardo Angulo, chairman of the Salem–Keizer Coalition for Equality, a civil rights group, said,

> The problem we're having are kids in the fifth, sixth, seventh grades that are reading and writing two or three grades behind. They're targets of the gang

Culture of the Streets

Experts attributed the rise in the murder rate among African-American youths to the culture of the streets, noting there were few diversions in their neighborhoods to help keep them out of trouble. Carnegie Mellon University criminology professor Alfred Blumstein said, "In the inner city, you have large numbers of kids with no future, hanging out together with a great emphasis on their street credibility. They'll go to great lengths to avenge an insult."[2]

Ten-year-old Faheem Thomas-Childs was shot and killed in gang cross fire outside his school in Philadelphia in 2004.

culture because these kids feel there is not much incentive for them to be in school. The gang culture is recruiting those kids that are still looking for a place to fit.[3]

Gang members have high dropout rates from school. Without enough education, they face lifetimes of low wages if they do—or are able to—quit their gangs. But without a high school diploma and the skills they need to succeed, gang members are less likely to leave the gang. This creates a vicious circle.

School officials struggle with how to reach students before they join gangs or, if they are members, how to curb violence in schools. Salem schools have made a rule against wearing gang colors on school property, but fights still persist. Gang members are still well aware of who belongs to which gangs.

Salem Police Sergeant Doug Carpenter said that fights can disrupt the school day at almost any time. A minor problem between two gang members can quickly escalate into a full-scale battle. Gang members use their cell phones to text one another, alerting everyone in the gang to the fight. Even calling gang members into the school office presents a problem. School officials are concerned that if they summon rival gang members to the office at the same time, a melee could break

Gangs in Salem Schools

A 2008 study by the Salem, Oregon, city schools found that 17 percent of middle school students had been invited to join gangs, and 10 percent had carried weapons into schools. The prior year, Salem school officials concluded that 14 percent of high school sophomores came to school carrying guns.

out. Even a fight off school grounds affects the school day. "These kids come to school scared, or they're talking about what happened in the neighborhood," said Carpenter. "They're not learning anything."[4]

Graffiti has also become a problem in Salem schools. The school district has been forced to assign two employees full-time to cleaning school walls.

Murder Rate Rises

As Jamiel Shaw's death illustrates, gangs rob society of vital young people who have no connection to gang violence. As for the gang members themselves, many will ultimately spend most of their adult lives in prison, serving time for violent crimes. And they may be the lucky ones. Very often, young people pay a much steeper price for gang membership: they are killed or severely injured in territory battles.

Gangs and Guns

The FBI reported that gangs are increasingly using guns in their criminal activities. As of 2007, 94 percent of gang-related murders involved the use of a gun. Gangs often obtain firearms through theft or illegal purchases from other gangs. In 2008, Los Angeles police arrested Crips and Bloods gang members for illegally selling more than 100 firearms.

In 2008, Northeastern University in Boston released a study. It reported that since 2000, the murder rate among African-American youths rose 34 percent, while violent crime remained, overall, relatively steady. Authors of the report blamed gang activity as a primary cause for the increase. Alfred Blumstein, Carnegie Mellon University criminology professor, stated,

> *The aggregate national murder rate since 2000 has been impressively flat—not to say there haven't been fluctuations in individual cities. But when you see a spike in a city, it very often involves young black males shooting other young black males.*[5]

Subtle Consequences

Murder and other violent acts may be the most obvious consequence of

Hope amid Violence

Although crime continues to increase in many cities with gang activity, federal and local authorities are still confident that vigilant, cooperative efforts will eventually reduce crime. In his closing statement to a 2008 summit on U.S. gang activity, FBI Deputy Director John S. Pistole said, "No matter how formidable the challenges we face—no matter how forcefully gang violence threatens to tear our communities and our coalitions asunder—we must maintain our commitment to being neighbors, friends, partners, and allies. Standing together, we are more formidable than any adversary. And standing together, we will prevail."[6]

A Bloods leader shows some of his gunshot scars.
He has been shot 23 times.

gangs. However, gangs produce more subtle negative effects on society.

Many members who quit their gangs find the process of reforming their lives very difficult. While they may have good intentions to become positive members of society, their earlier involvement in gangs serves as a great challenge to bettering their lives. For example, they often have criminal records that prohibit them from getting jobs or housing.

Communities, and gang members themselves, also suffer from the lost potential surrounding the gang culture. When young people join gangs, they are giving up healthy and constructive activities that could improve their lives and their communities.

Many gang members continue to brush up against the criminal justice system throughout their lives. California attorney general Edmund G. Brown Jr. stated in a report,

> *Belonging to a gang severely harms a young person's future. Gang members often socialize only with other gang members, reinforcing their limited view of life. They frequently establish a lifelong pattern of involvement with the criminal justice system. They may commit serious and violent crimes that lead to lengthy incarcerations.*[7]

Edmund G. Brown Jr.

Edmund G. Brown Jr. served as governor of California from 1975 to 1983. As governor, Brown enacted a "use a gun, go to prison" law to curb gun-related violence. He also started several programs that took tough aim at gangs and gang culture, including the Career Criminal Prosecution Program, the Career Criminal Apprehension Program, and the Crime Resistance Task Force.

In 1992, Brown campaigned for the Democratic presidential nomination against Bill Clinton. In 1998, Brown was elected mayor of Oakland, California, where one of his three main goals was to reduce crime in the city. As of his eighth year as mayor in 2006, Oakland crime had dropped 30 percent. In 2006, Brown became California's attorney general, the chief law enforcement officer for the state.

Often, gang members spend time in jail in one form or another—whether on short-term or life sentences. It costs money to keep inmates in prison. The added expense of prison costs, in addition to increased police units and task forces and the strain on the justice system, are consequences of gang violence and gang culture.

Weapons seized in a raid on a Los Angeles gang in 2005

An arrested Mara Salvatrucha gang member in 2006

COMMUNITIES TAKE ACTION

Numerous officials take a tough attitude against gangs. They believe the best way to stop gang activity is to throw gang leaders in jail. State and federal legislators have adopted laws and investigative techniques specifically designed to stem gang activities. Still, many believe arresting and sentencing gang members is not enough.

After a series of drive-by shootings in the towns of Sunnyside and Grandview, Washington, community members staged a rally. More than 200 residents of the two towns marched to a park in Sunnyside. Amid rousing speeches, the protesters demanded action against gangs. Community leaders in Sunnyside and Grandview took action. They organized a group, Grandview United, to develop programs that would divert young people from gangs, lobby state legislators for tougher antigang laws, and form neighborhood watch groups to alert police about gang activities.

Like Sunnyside and Grandview, many communities have crafted strategies to address gang problems. Diverting current or potential gang

Are Parents Too Lax?

Linda Schmidt, a community outreach specialist for the FBI and an expert on gangs, believes parents can go a long way toward helping their children stay out of gangs. She says that parents need to keep a closer watch over their children. She says, "One of the attractions of a gang is its strict discipline. With that discipline comes structure and limits and a sense of security and belonging. That's what we need to offer to our young people as well—just in a positive way. We can't be afraid, as parents and teachers, to provide structure and discipline to our children and students."[1]

members into positive activities may be one solution to curbing gang violence.

The RICO Act

One national study published in 2006 concluded that 13 percent of U.S. prison inmates belonged to gangs. Such statistics suggest that police and prosecutors have made good use of the legal system to sweep gang members off the streets.

One effective law in combating gangs has been the U.S. Racketeer Influenced and Corrupt Organizations Act (RICO). Congress adopted RICO in 1970 to give federal agents and prosecutors a strong weapon to use against drug-trafficking kingpins. The law was based on the concept that simply profiting from the activities of a criminal organization is a crime. Prior to RICO, prosecutors had to prove that mobsters actually pulled the trigger or sold the drugs. With RICO, it is enough for prosecutors to prove that the mob members received payment from the activities of their organizations.

However, until 2001, RICO was rarely used to prosecute street gang members. That year, federal prosecutors started using RICO against street gangs with significant success. Since then, nearly 400 gang members have been prosecuted under RICO. John S. Pistole of the FBI stated,

> *Our strategy has been to eliminate the leadership of gang enterprises. Our goal is not just to disrupt their activities, but dismantle them entirely.*
>
> *Taking apart a gang is like demolishing a building. Hacking away at individual walls and beams might damage the building, but it doesn't destroy it. But using federal drug and racketeering statutes is akin to dynamiting the foundation. Once the gang's leadership infrastructure implodes, all members are weakened. It becomes difficult for the group to operate. Eventually, it crumbles.*
>
> *And so our strategy is to prosecute as many gang leaders, members, and associates as possible so there are no pieces left which are large enough to allow the gang to rebuild.* [2]

Banning Gangs in Ventura County

Authorities in Ventura County, California, have banned gang members from assembling, wearing gang colors, and flashing gang signs within a 6.6-square-mile (17-square-km) zone where gang activity has been high. The ban is aimed at controlling the Colonia Chiques, a gang with approximately 1,000 members in the area. "I consider this to be a victory for law enforcement in controlling gangs," said Michael Schwartz, a Ventura County special assistant district attorney. [3]

YEAR	ARRESTS	CONVICTIONS
2001	3,999	2,168
2002	3,512	1,964
2003	3,837	1,698
2004	4,162	1,773
2005	4,745	1,700
2006	5,537	2,199
2007	7,256	2,325
2008	2,385	1,427
TOTALS	**35,433**	**15,254**

Arrests and convictions by Safe Streets Task Forces throughout the United States

OTHER STRATEGIES

Authorities have also formed Safe Streets Task Forces. These task forces employ local and state police as well as federal agents who pool their resources to fight gang-related crime. Typically, the task forces combine the expertise of local police officers, who best know their streets, with sophisticated wiretapping devices and other electronic resources from the FBI.

By 2008, the FBI and local police forces had established more than 140 gang task forces in 40 states as well as Puerto Rico and the U.S. Virgin Islands. Task forces are working in such diverse communities as Palm Beach, Florida, and Conasauga, Georgia, as well as major cities such as Detroit, Chicago, New York City, and Los Angeles. "This is the kind of coordination we need to confront gang violence. When your cities face a rash of homicides or armed robberies, you have to act quickly," Pistole said. "Your immediate concern is making sure the gang members don't get away with murder—or think they have—and become emboldened to commit more crimes."[4]

Another strategy is to prosecute gang members in federal courts, where sentences for criminal activities are often much longer than in local courts. In suburban Philadelphia, Terror Dome Kings member Joshua Newkirk had been convicted in a local court on a drug-dealing charge and sentenced to 14 months in prison. When Newkirk was released, he allegedly returned to dealing drugs. The next time Newkirk was arrested, he was charged in a federal court. In 2009, he faced a potential sentence of 15 years in prison. Moreover, Newkirk faced judgment as a "career offender," which could lead to a life sentence.

Operation Ceasefire

Prosecutors' and law enforcement agencies' tough attitudes against gang leaders has become increasingly more effective. But while tens of thousands of gang members sit in prison cells, many serving life terms, others soon fill their places in the gangs.

Many gang experts advocate what is known as the "Operation Ceasefire"

Antigraffiti Campaigns

Many communities have adopted tough attitudes toward graffiti by passing stiff ordinances against tagging. In Renton, Washington, the town council ruled that parents must pay for the cleanup if their children are charged with defacing public property. The town has also made cleaning supplies available free of charge to business owners. It has organized volunteer squads who scrub walls and placed security cameras around town, all in an effort to catch taggers in the act.

In other communities, laws require retailers to keep cans of spray paint and permanent markers in locked cabinets. This is to discourage shoplifting by gang members looking for graffiti supplies. Some city governments have established hotlines and provide residents with numbers to call if they see a gang member or other perpetrator in the act of tagging a wall. Some cities have deployed antigraffiti teams to scrape and wash paint off walls. Often the teams are composed of a city worker supervising convicted gang members who have been ordered to perform the community service. "When they clean it up, they don't want to write graffiti," said Vanessa Branco, a leader of the United 40s, a New York City civic association.[5]

approach, which was first tried in Boston in the 1990s. Under Operation Ceasefire, authorities take a stern attitude toward gang violence. At the same time, they meet one-on-one with gang members to convince them to turn in their guns. Authorities make it clear to gang members that they will continue arresting and prosecuting them until the violence stops.

Under Operation Ceasefire, diversionary programs are offered to potential gang members. The hope is to steer them away from gang culture before they are given a chance to join. Schools, churches, recreational centers, and other community groups are urged to establish after-school programs where young people can gather for constructive purposes.

In Boston, Operation Ceasefire was judged a success—youth homicides decreased by 63 percent in just a few years. However,

Gang Violence Down in San Jose

Gang violence decreased significantly in San Jose, California, after the city established a gang-prevention program that would cost $6 million in two years. In addition to efforts to target and arrest gang leaders, San Jose established the Summer Safety Initiative program. This program provides young people with activities to keep them busy during summer, such as field trips, block parties, movie nights, visits to college campuses, and carnivals. Participants can also take part in sports, plays, and art projects, and counselors help them learn decision-making skills. In 2008, after just one year of the program, San Jose officials reported a 16-percent drop in gang-related violent crime and a 30-percent drop in gang-related nonviolent crime, which includes drug offenses.

authorities have found that there is no single answer to eliminating gang involvement in all communities. Because each community and gang is unique, approaches to deterring gang involvement must be tailored to specific locations.

Former First Lady Laura Bush talks at a Ceasefire event. The organization works to stop gang violence before it starts.

Former gang member Mike Cummings helps students who live in a gang-infested neighborhood of Los Angeles make it to school safely.

LIFE AFTER A GANG

onrad Harris joined the Bloods in junior high school. Soon, he started selling drugs. The first time he was arrested, he was 21 years old. Convicted of selling cocaine, he was sentenced to four years in prison.

In jail, he met some Crips serving their own prison terms. He had considered the Crips his longtime enemies. However, in prison he learned that he shared a lot in common with his rivals. He said, "I started looking at it like, 'Wow man, these dudes ain't all that bad. They people just like me. They got problems just like me.'"[1] Harris left prison with a different outlook on the Crips, but he still returned to gang life. He started selling drugs again and was arrested a second time. This time, the judge sentenced him to ten years in prison.

During his second incarceration, Harris shared a cell with Percy Jenkins, who had been in prison since 1972 and was serving a life term. Harris said Jenkins influenced him to change his life when he said,

> *If you leave . . . these walls the same person you was when you came in, you going to come back to the same situation. It don't change. . . . You got to change yourself if you expect to do any changing in your life. If not, you're going to be up in here with a life sentence like me.*[2]

During his two jail terms, Harris learned some valuable lessons. He had no good reason to hate rival gang members. And if he continued in a gang, he would end up in prison for the rest of his life.

LEAVING A GANG

Like Conrad Harris, some gang members ultimately decide that gang life is not for them. In some cases, they undergo bad experiences, such as being shot or sent to jail. Afterward, they may realize that if they stay in the gang they will either be killed or imprisoned again—probably for many years or even life.

Other members say they simply outgrow gang culture. They resolve to take responsibility for their own lives and the lives of family members. Perhaps they have become parents and do not want their children to grow up the way they did. This realization may encourage them to quit their gangs, return to school, or find jobs. After leaving his gang, Kershaun Scott moved his family to Ridgecrest, a desert town approximately 150 miles (240 km) north of his former gang territory in Los Angeles.

Scared Straight

A 1978 documentary titled *Scared Straight* is given credit for reha-bilitating countless gang members. Filmed at a New Jersey state prison, the movie depicts hard-ened criminals berating a group of young gang members, warning them to give up their lives of crime. The film won an Academy Award as the year's best documen-tary. Since its release, many states have devel-oped their own "Scared Straight" programs, using inmate volunteers to warn young people who have gotten in trouble with the law. A sequel, filmed in 1999, showed that most of the gang members who participated in the 1978 version did turn their lives around.

Gangs

Sometimes, a member cannot simply walk away from his gang. Many gangs require members to be "beaten out" of the gang. This means they must fight their way out. When Phong Tran turned 21, he told members of his Bloods gang from Revere, Massachusetts, that he intended to quit. On his birthday, Tran was approached by two other Bloods. Suddenly, one of them struck Tran in the head with a bottle. "You want out now, Blood?" one of the assailants taunted.[3] Tran lost three pints of blood in the assault and required 30 staples

Jobs for Former Gang Members

Former gang members often have trouble finding work. But if they live in Los Angeles, they may find a willing employer at Homeboy Industries. Gregory Boyle, a Catholic priest, founded the company in 1992. It hires former gang members in a number of businesses, including a bakery, restaurant, T-shirt silk-screening plant, and retail store.

When Boyle was assigned to a parish in a gang-infested neighborhood, he tried to convince local businesses to hire former gang members. When his efforts fell short, he resolved to start his own business as a way of finding jobs for the young men. Ray Stark, a Hollywood producer, donated a building for the enterprise.

Boyle put six former gang members to work renovating the building, which they turned into a bakery. The bakery now employs 25 former gang members, and dozens more work in other Homeboy businesses. Many of Homeboy's employees have left the company to find jobs elsewhere. Gabriel Flores, a former gang member who works as a silk-screener, stated, "When I got that first paycheck . . . it made me feel good. I didn't steal a car or sell drugs for the money. I worked for it."[4]

to close the wound in his face. By taking the beating, though, Tran was permitted to leave the Bloods.

Other gang members insist that having to endure a beating to leave a gang is rare. Sociologists who interviewed former gang members in Denver, Colorado, found that two-thirds of them were able to walk away from their gangs without having to fend off violent attacks. Many also said they simply moved away, either to new neighborhoods or different states. Only two former gang members reported having been formally beaten out of their gangs. The Justice Policy Institute, a Washington-based organization that studies criminal justice issues, added,

> *The principal barrier to leaving a gang is not fear of punishment by the gang but the difficulty many gang members face when they try to make new lives for themselves. . . . Mainstream social institutions are reluctant to embrace former gang members. Thus former gang members experience the worst of both worlds: "After all, what incentive is there to leave the gang when it is the source of their friends and when past criminal activities committed as gang members cause many groups to treat them as if they remained in the gang?"[5]*

Greg Boyle, left, with former gang members at the Homeboy Industries headquarters in Los Angeles

A HARSH REALITY

Ex-gang members face the harsh reality that starting to live life in a positive way may be difficult. The overwhelming task can be a reason to remain in a gang.

Juan Rivera joined the *Mesa Locos* gang in Oceanside, California, at the age of 12. Over the next dozen years, he was arrested and incarcerated many times. Finally, at the end of a 19-month prison

Removing Tattoos

Tattoos are a big part of gang culture. Former gang members know their tattoos can often stand in the way of finding jobs and turning their lives around. Tattoo removal can be painful and expensive. The markings are burned off with a laser, and it usually takes several treatments. At Long Beach Memorial Medical Center in California, physicians provide free tattoo removal for former gang members under a program known as "Erasing the Past." Former gang member Angel Usi Jr. had so many tattoos that he had to endure more than 40 painful laser treatments. Usi said it was worth it. "Once a treatment is done, you feel better about yourself, especially when you look in the mirror," he said. "Most people, when they make a change, change an outfit or cut their hair. This is drastic. This is a new beginning for me."[6]

term, he resolved to quit the gang and turn his life around.

After his release, his first notion was to join the military. He was turned down by a Marine recruiter who explained that his long affiliation with the gang and criminal record disqualified him from military service. When Rivera applied for a job at a supermarket, the manager looked at the gang-related tattoos covering Rivera's arms and neck and told him he had no job to offer. Since his release from prison, Rivera has been able to find only part-time work as a carpenter. Rivera realizes his past as a gang member has made it very difficult for him to find work, but he is determined to keep trying.

RESPONSIBILITY TO THEIR COMMUNITIES

Many former gang members feel a responsibility to help their communities, usually by joining gang–intervention programs. After leaving jail and quitting the Bloods, Conrad Harris became a board member of the Overcoming Gangs organization based in San Diego. He counsels gang members and helps them find jobs and career training. He also coaches football and serves on a city commission that addresses gang issues. Harris says that giving his time is a small price to pay for the wrong he created in his community.

Conrad Harris, Juan Rivera, Kershaun Scott, and others prove there can be life after gangs. The fates of other gang members, including Kershaun's brother, Kody, illustrate the difficulty of breaking away from gang culture. Furthermore, gang violence affects entire communities. Schools and neighborhoods deteriorate, and innocent people suffer. Some of them, such as Jamiel Shaw, have paid the ultimate price.

Injunctions

Starting in the 1990s, Los Angeles police employed the strategy of obtaining injunctions against suspected gang members. Injunctions are court orders that bar the members from associating with others in gangs, loitering in public, and violating laws. The injunctions have been effective because gang members could be imprisoned for violating them. However, many ex-gang members have found that the injunctions have caused obstacles for them long after they left their gangs. When prospective employers perform background checks, they find the injunctions and decide not to make offers of employment. Advocates for the former gang members have called for the city to withdraw many of the injunctions.

Council for Unity

Founded in 1975 by former gang member Bob De Sena, the New York-based Council for Unity is credited with steering some 100,000 young people away from gangs. The council operates a number of educational and counseling programs. Its main goal is to bring rival gang members together to show them they have nothing to fear from one another.

Many of the group's counselors are former gang members. Sean Johnson spent years in a New York State prison on drug charges. After his release, he became a counselor for the organization. Johnson said of the men he works with, "When they see someone who's been to hell and back, it clicks: 'If he can do it, I can do it.'"[8]

What can communities do to limit gangs? As they struggle for the answer, they may do well to heed the words of former gang member Conrad Harris:

You have to get to these kids as early as eight all the way up through nineteen, twenty, twenty-one. Once that child walks out of that house you can still have some type of positive effect on them no matter how [bad] the home is.[7]

Former gang member Albert Juarez encourages gang members to leave
their gangs and return to school.

TIMELINE

1788	1910	1920
Early U.S. gang leaders Levi and Abraham Doan are hanged.	The Mexican Revolution begins. Mexican families immigrate to the United States, where their sons form the first Latino gangs.	On January 16, Prohibition begins. It fosters bootlegging, which elevates street gangs into major criminal organizations.

1971	1970s	1978
Stanley "Tookie" Williams merges his gang with Raymond Washington's gang to form the Crips.	The Bloods form in Compton, California, as rivals to the Crips.	The documentary film *Scared Straight* is released.

1933

On December 5, Prohibition is repealed; bootleggers turn to gambling, drug trafficking, and prostitution.

1943

On June 3, after white sailors attack Latino gang members, the zoot suit riots erupt in Los Angeles.

1970

Congress passes the Racketeer Influenced and Corrupt Organizations Act (RICO).

1989

The rap group NWA releases the album *Straight Outta Compton*, establishing gangsta rap as a genre of popular music.

1992

Gregory Boyle establishes Homeboy Industries to give former gang members jobs.

1993

Kody Scott publishes *Monster: The Autobiography of an L.A. Gang Member*, chronicling his life in the Crips.

TIMELINE

1996

Boston police
initiate Operation
Ceasefire to divert
young people away
from gangs.

2001

Federal officials
start using RICO
to prosecute drug-
trafficking kingpins.

2005

On December 13,
Tookie Williams is
executed in California
for committing
four murders.

2006

Harry S. Truman High
School class president
Tyrone Lewis gives
his commencement
address by satellite
to escape gang
retaliation.

2003

Hollenbeck, a
neighborhood in
Los Angeles, has
an estimated gang
population of 6,800
young people.

2003

Gang members
commit 6.5 percent
of all murders in
the United States.

2008

More than 140
Safe Streets Task
Forces operate in
the United States,
Puerto Rico, and the
U.S. Virgin Islands.

2008

Jamiel Shaw, a star
high school football
player, is murdered
by a member of the
18th Street gang.

ESSENTIAL FACTS

AT ISSUE

❖ Gangs related to organized crime began to grow in the United States in the early twentieth century as crime became big business for groups such as the Mafia.

❖ Young people join gangs for many reasons. Their motives may be to make money, gain respect, be among members of their own ethnic group, or to experience a feeling of belonging that they may be missing at home. Also, some young people who live in gang-infested neighborhoods join gangs because they see no other option.

❖ Gangs affect all areas of the United States, including both coasts and the interior of the country, urban and rural areas, and affluent and poverty-stricken cities.

❖ Law enforcement officials and community agencies have taken active steps to counteract gang culture. The FBI shares its resources with local authorities to combat criminal activity. Communities run programs that offer positive activities for at-risk youth.

❖ Gang culture affects not only gang members and the victims of their crimes but entire communities. In areas with high gang activity, residents live in fear. Businesses are less likely to operate, leaving the neighborhood in poverty. Communities also suffer from the loss of gang members' potential.

CRITICAL DATES

1971
The Crips formed on the West Coast. Soon after, the Bloods formed as their rivals. This signaled the beginning of violent gang rivalries.

1992
Gregory Boyle, a Catholic priest, founded Homeboy Industries as a business for former gang members to gain employment.

1996

Boston police began Operation Ceasefire, a program that urged current gang members to stop their criminal lives and developed programs to steer young people away from joining gangs. Youth homicides in the area decreased by 63 percent a few years after the program began.

2008

A member of the 18th Street gang murdered Jamiel Shaw, a high-school football star with no gang affiliations. This incident shocked the community and reminded many that the consequences of gangs reach beyond the individual groups.

QUOTES

"What distinguishes the most deeply involved gang members from peers is a worldview in which fighting is a normal part of life and the rules of mainstream society do not fully apply."—*Justice Policy Institute*

"Belonging to a gang severely harms a young person's future. Gang members often socialize only with other gang members, reinforcing their limited view of life. They frequently establish a lifelong pattern of involvement with the criminal justice system. They may commit serious and violent crimes that lead to lengthy incarcerations."—*Edmund G. Brown Jr., California attorney general*

ADDITIONAL RESOURCES

SELECT BIBLIOGRAPHY

Greene, Judith, and Kevin Pranis. *Gang Wars: The Failure of Enforcement Tactics and the Need for Effective Public Safety Strategies*. Washington DC: Justice Policy Institute. July 2007.

Hagedorn, John M. *A World of Gangs: Armed Young Men and Gangsta Culture*. Minneapolis, MN: University of Minnesota Press, 2008.

Shakur, Sanyika. *Monster: The Autobiography of an L.A. Gang Member*. New York, NY: Grove Press, 1993.

Simpson, Colton, and Ann Pearlman. *Inside the Crips: Life Inside L.A.'s Most Notorious Gang*. New York, NY: St. Martin's Griffin, 2006.

FURTHER READING

Black, Andy. *Organized Crime*. Broomall, PA: Mason Crest Publishers, 2003.

Jackson, Robert K., and Wesley D. McBride. *Understanding Street Gangs*. Incline Village, NV: Cooperhouse Publishing Company, 1996.

Newton, Michael. *Gangs and Gang Crime*. New York, NY: Chelsea House, 2008.

Ojeda, Auriana, ed. *Juvenile Crime: Opposing Viewpoints*. San Diego, CA: Greenhaven Press, 2002.

WEB LINKS

To learn more about gangs, visit ABDO Publishing Company online at **www.abdopublishing.com**. Web sites about gangs are featured on our Book Links page. These links are routinely monitored and updated to provide the most current information available.

For More Information

For more information on this subject, contact or visit the following organizations.

Federal Bureau of Investigation
J. Edgar Hoover Building, 935 Pennsylvania Avenue Northwest, Washington, DC 20535-0001
202-324-3000
www.fbi.gov
The FBI has made many of its resources available to local and state police agencies to help them combat gang activity. Visitors to the Web site can learn more about what their area is doing to prohibit gang activity.

Homeboy Industries
130 West Bruno Street, Los Angeles, CA 90012
323-526-1254
www.homeboy-industries.org
Homeboy Industries operates a bakery, retail store, T-shirt silk-screening factory, and other businesses that employ former gang members. Visitors to the Web site can find more information about each of the Homeboy businesses.

Glossary

baby G
   A new recruit to a gang, often as young as ten or eleven.

bootleggers
   Criminals who made and sold liquor illegally.

delinquent
   In violation of the law.

graffiti
   Messages painted on outdoor walls; sometimes they mark gang territory and/or convey messages about gang activity.

incarcerate
   To put in prison.

injunction
   A court order that prohibits an action.

jumping in
   An initiation rite requiring a prospective gang member to prove his toughness by allowing himself to be beaten up by other gang members.

kingpin
   The chief person of an organization.

Mafia
   A Sicilian criminal organization.

melee
   A confused fight.

O.G.
Initials that stand for "original gangster," who is the head of a street gang or set.

ordinance
A law.

Prohibition
The period of time in the United States (1920–1933) during which it was illegal to consume or sell alcohol.

racketeer
A person who receives money from illegal activities.

set
A single street gang affiliated with a national gang.

sociologist
A professional who studies the development of human society.

tagging
Spreading graffiti throughout a gang's neighborhood.

warrant
A document that gives authorities the right to make an arrest, a search, or a seizure.

SOURCE NOTES

Chapter 1. Two Gang Members
1. Sanyika Shakur. *Monster: The Autobiography of an L.A. Gang Member*. New York: Grove Press, 1993. 6–7.
2. Ibid. 52.
3. Mandalit del Barco. "Gang Member Turned Author Arrested in L.A." National Public Radio. 9 Mar. 2007. 12 Feb. 2009 <http://www.npr.org/templates/story/story.php?storyId=7793148>.
4. Jeffrey Anderson. "No Escape for an O.G." *LA Weekly*. 29 Jan. 2004. 12 Feb. 2009 <http://www.laweekly.com/2004-01-29/news/no-escape-for-an-o-g>.
5. Susan Faludi. "Ghetto Star: 'Monster' Kody Scott and the Culture of Ornament." *LA Weekly*. 14 Oct. 1999. 12 Feb. 2009 <http://www.laweekly.com/1999-10-14/news/ghetto-star>.
6. Kershaun Scott. "Monster Rap: An Ex-Gangbanger's Take on Stemming the Violence." *LA Weekly*. 12 Dec. 2002. 12 Feb. 2009 <http://www.laweekly.com/2002-12-12/news/monster-rap>.
7. John S. Pistole. "2nd Los Angeles IACP Summit on Transnational Gangs." FBI.gov. 3 March 2008. 12 Feb. 2009 <http://www.fbi.gov/pressrel/speeches/pistole030308.htm>.
8. Colton Simpson and Ann Pearlman. *Inside the Crips: Life Inside L.A.'s Most Notorious Gang*. New York: St. Martin's Griffin, 2006. xxi.

Chapter 2. A History of Gangs
1. Jacob A. Riis. *How the Other Half Lives: Studies Among the Tenements of New York*. New York: Charles A. Scribner's Sons, 1890. 218.
2. Susan Ferriss and Ricardo Sandoval. *The Fight in the Fields: Cesar Chavez and the Farmworkers Movement*. New York: Harcourt Brace & Company, 1997. 44.
3. Jacob A. Riis. *How the Other Half Lives: Studies Among the Tenements of New York*. New York: Charles A. Scribner's Sons, 1890. 217.

Chapter 3. Gang Networks
1. John M. Hagedorn. *A World of Gangs: Armed Young Men and Gangsta Culture*. Minneapolis, MN: University of Minnesota Press, 2008. 9.
2. Joe Vazquez. "Gangs Turn to Social Networking Sites to Recruit." KPIX TV. 7 Feb. 2008. 12 Feb. 2009 <http://cbs5.com/local/Internet.gang.recruiting.2.648038.html>.

Chapter 4. Why Young People Join Gangs
1. Lauren Crecelius. "Gang Busters: Seeking Solutions in Santa Barbara." University of California-Santa Barbara *Daily Nexus*. 14 Feb. 2008. 12 Feb. 2009 <http://www.dailynexus.com/article.php?a=15852>.

2. Judith Greene and Kevin Pranis. *Gang Wars: The Failure of Enforcement Tactics and the Need for Effective Public Safety Strategies*. Washington DC: Justice Policy Institute. July 2007. 46.

3. Edmund G. Brown Jr. *Gangs: A Community Response*. Sacramento, CA: California Attorney General's Office, 2003. 30.

4. Charles P. Cozic, ed. *Gangs: Opposing Viewpoints*. San Diego, CA: Greenhaven Press, 1996. 155.

5. Judith Greene and Kevin Pranis. *Gang Wars: The Failure of Enforcement Tactics and the Need for Effective Public Safety Strategies*. Washington DC: Justice Policy Institute. July 2007. 45.

6. Colton Simpson and Ann Pearlman. *Inside the Crips: Life Inside L.A.'s Most Notorious Gang*. New York: St. Martin's Griffin, 2006. 20.

7. Susan Faludi. "Ghetto Star: 'Monster' Kody Scott and the Culture of Ornament." *LA Weekly*. 14 Oct. 1999. 12 Feb. 2009 <http://www.laweekly.com/1999-10-14/news/ghetto-star>.

8. Danielle Ameden. "Police: Ashland Stabbing a Gang-Initiation Ritual." *MetroWest Daily News*. 7 Oct. 2007. 12 Feb. 2009 <http://www.metrowestdailynews.com/homepage/x1498614554>.

9. Martin Sanchez Jankowski. *Islands in the Street: Gangs and American Society*. Berkeley, CA: University of California Press, 1991. 107.

Chapter 5. Gangs and Crime

1. Derrick Watkins and Richard Ashby. *Gang Investigations*. Sudbury, MA: Jones and Bartlett, 2007. 36.

2. Charles P. Cozic, ed. *Gangs: Opposing Viewpoints*. San Diego, CA: Greenhaven Press, 1996. 171.

3. John M. Hagedorn. *A World of Gangs: Armed Young Men and Gangsta Culture*. Minneapolis, MN: University of Minnesota Press, 2008. 97.

4. "Former Gang Member 'El Cholo' Speaks Out." National Public Radio. 27 Dec. 2008. 12 Feb. 2009 <http://www.npr.org/templates/story/story.php?storyId=98598356>.

5. Sanyika Shakur. *Monster: The Autobiography of an L.A. Gang Member*. New York: Grove Press, 1993. 17.

Chapter 6. Gangs outside Big Cities

1. Ross Courtney. "Lower Valley Residents March Against Gangs." *Yakima Herald-Republic*. 25 Oct. 2008. 12 Feb. 2009 <http://www.yakima-herald.com/stories/2008/10/25/lower-valley-residents-march-against-gangs>.

2. Mark Sappenfield. "Gang Colors Flourish in Farm Country." *Christian Science Monitor*. 1 Oct. 2001. 12 Feb. 2009 <http://www.csmonitor.com/2001/1001/p3s1-ussc.html>.

Source Notes Continued

3. Tim Reiterman. "Small Towns, Big Gang Issues." *Los Angeles Times*. 24 Feb. 2008. 12 Feb. 2009 <http://articles.latimes.com/2008/feb/24/local/me-gangs24>.

4. Ibid.

5. David Kocieniewski. "After Gang Threat, It's Cap, Gown and Lockdown." *New York Times*. 10 June 2006. 12 Feb. 2009 <http://www.nytimes.com/2006/06/10/nyregion/10graduate.html>.

6. Michael Ferraresi. "Gang's Rise Unnerves Local Police." *Arizona Republic*. 5 Oct. 2008.

7. Melinda Henneberger. "Gang Membership Grows in Middle-Class Suburbs." *New York Times*. 24 July 1993. 1-A.

8. David Kocieniewski. "After Gang Threat, It's Cap, Gown and Lockdown." *New York Times*. 10 June 2006. 12 Feb. 2009 <http://www.nytimes.com/2006/06/10/nyregion/10graduate.html>.

Chapter 7. The Consequences of Gangs

1. "L.A. Police: Gang Member Charged With Murder in High School Football Star's Death." Fox News. 12 Mar. 2008. 12 Feb. 2009 <http://www.foxnews.com/story/0,2933,336834,00.html>.

2. Erik Eckholm. "Murders by Black Teenagers Rise, Bucking a Trend." *New York Times*. 29 Dec. 2008. A-12.

3. Tracy Loew and Ruth Liao. "Pervasive Spread of Gang Culture Makes Youths Vulnerable." *Oregon Statesman Journal*. 21 Dec. 2008. 12 Feb. 2009 <http://www.statesmanjournal.com/article/20081221/NEWS/812210315>.

4. Ibid.

5. Erik Eckholm. "Murders by Black Teenagers Rise, Bucking a Trend." *New York Times*. 29 Dec. 2008. A-12.

6. John S. Pistole. "2nd Los Angeles IACP Summit on Transnational Gangs." FBI.gov. 3 March 2008. 12 Feb. 2009 <http://www.fbi.gov/pressrel/speeches/pistole030308.htm>.

7. Edmund G. Brown Jr. *Gangs: A Community Response*. Sacramento, CA: California Attorney General's Office, 2003. 1.

Chapter 8. Communities Take Action

1. Linda Schmidt. "Words of Advice from an Expert on Street Gangs." FBI.gov. 10 July 2008. 12 Feb. 2009 <http://www.fbi.gov/page2/july08/gangs_071008.html>.

2. John S. Pistole. "2nd Los Angeles IACP Summit on Transnational Gangs." FBI.gov. 3 Mar. 2008. 12 Feb. 2009 <http://www.fbi.gov/pressrel/speeches/pistole030308.htm>.

3. Gregory W. Griggs. "Most of Gang Ban is Upheld." *Los Angeles Times*. 17 Oct. 2007. B-4.

4. John S. Pistole. "2nd Los Angeles IACP Summit on Transnational Gangs." FBI.gov. 3 Mar. 2008. 12 Feb. 2009 <http://www.fbi.gov/pressrel/speeches/pistole030308.htm>.

5. Oren Yaniv. "Anti-Graffiti Team Targets Taggers." *New York Daily News*. 11 Feb. 2005. 12 Feb. 2009 <https://www.nydailynews.com/archives/ny_local/2005/02/01/2005-02-01_anti-graffiti_team_targeting.html>.

Chapter 9. Life after a Gang

1. Daniel Strumpf. "After Gang Life: Questions for Conrad Harris." *voiceofsandiego.org Online*. 8 Dec. 2006. 12 Feb. 2009 <http://www.voiceofsandiego.org/articles/2006/12/08/education/featured_stories/01harris.txt>.

2. Ibid.

3. Jay Atkinson. "Police Setting Up Database on Gangs." *Boston Globe*. 30 Nov. 2008. 12 Feb. 2009 <http://www.boston.com/news/local/massachusetts/articles/2008/11/30/police_setting_up_database_on_gangs/>.

4. Edward Iwata. "Homeboy Industries Goes Gang-Busters; L.A. Group Helps Former Gang Members Get Jobs—and Hope." *USA Today*. 11 July 2005. B-1.

5. Judith Greene and Kevin Pranis. *Gang Wars: The Failure of Enforcement Tactics and the Need for Effective Public Safety Strategies*. Washington DC: Justice Policy Institute. July 2007. 49.

6. Phillip Zonkel. "Long Beach Tattoo-Removal Program Helps Ex-Gang Members Build on Future." *Long Beach Press-Telegram*. 10 Dec. 2008. 12 Feb. 2009 <http://www.presstelegram.com/lifestyle/ci_11187322>.

7. Daniel Strumpf. "After Gang Life: Questions for Conrad Harris." *voiceofsandiego.org Online*. 8 Dec. 2006. 12 Feb. 2009 <http://www.voiceofsandiego.org/articles/2006/12/08/education/featured_stories/01harris.txt>.

8. Ula Ilnytzky, Associated Press. "Group Helps Gang Members Leave Crime." *USA Today*. 24 Mar. 2008. 12 Feb. 2009 <http://www.usatoday.com/news/nation/2008-03-24-1044761256_x.htm>.

INDEX

Los Norteños, 32, 58
Los Sureños, 31–32, 57

Mafia, 20–21
Mara Salvatrucha, 22–23, 30,
    49, 57
membership
    age of initiation, 23–24,
        38–39
    growth, 27
money, 17, 20, 36, 40–41, 49,
    55, 61, 74, 89
Monster: The Autobiography of an L.A.
    Gang Member, 11
murder, 8, 9, 13, 18, 20, 33,
    40, 50–51, 55, 61, 66, 67,
    70–71, 81

National Gang Intelligence
    Center, 47

Operation Ceasefire, 82–84
organization, 9–10, 11, 26–27
original gangster, 9–10, 11

Parker, Bonnie, 17
Pistole, John S., 14, 71, 79, 81
poverty, 38, 66, 67
prison, 11, 13, 20, 26, 33, 34,
    57, 58, 70, 73, 74, 78, 81,
    82, 86–88, 91–92, 93, 94.
    See also jail
Prohibition, 19–20

rap music, 13, 48
reputation, 7, 11, 36, 40, 61
RICO Act, 78–79

Riis, Jacob A., 18, 23
Rivera, John, 91–93
robbery, 7, 9, 11, 13, 16–17, 45,
    49–50, 60, 66, 81
Rollin' Sixties, 7–8
rural gangs, 13, 56–60

Safe Streets Task Forces, 80
Scared Straight, 88
schools, 6, 13, 38, 61, 67–70,
    83, 86, 88, 93
Scott, Kershaun, 8–9, 12–13,
    88, 93
Scott, Kody, 6–14, 40, 51, 93
Shaw, Jamiel, 64–65, 70, 93
shootings, 8–9, 55, 57, 66, 71,
    77
Simpson, Colton, 40, 49
Snoop Dogg, 48
State Street gang, 66
suburban gangs, 13, 56, 60–62
Sur 13. *See* Los Sureños

tattoos, 92
territory, 8, 9, 11, 28, 40, 58,
    59, 60, 65, 66–67, 70, 88
Tiny Rascals, 23, 33, 47
Tookie Speaks Out Against Gang
    Violence, 33
Twace, 48–49

Vice Lords, 32, 38, 60

Washington, Raymond, 27–28
white supremacy, 23
Williams, Stanley "Tookie," 28,
    33

ABOUT THE AUTHOR

Hal Marcovitz is a former newspaper reporter who has written more than 120 books for young readers. In 2005, *Nancy Pelosi*, his biography of House Speaker Nancy Pelosi, was named to *Booklist* magazine's list of recommended feminist books for young readers. As a journalist, he won three Keystone Press Awards, the highest award for newspaper reporting presented by the Pennsylvania Newspaper Association. He lives in Chalfont, Pennsylvania, with his wife and daughter.

PHOTO CREDITS